PRAISE FOR *A Field Guide to Relationships*

Christopher T. Rogers has written an eminently practical and engaging book about how to navigate the world of human relationships. Drawing on his professional experience as a counselor, Rogers provides the type of insight and perspective that can be understood and applied by anyone. It's not necessary to be in a relationship crisis to benefit from this book. But if a crisis exists or is looming on the horizon, open the cover as soon as possible!

Robert Whitlow, Best-selling author of *The List* and *Chosen People*

Reading through *A Field Guide to Relationships,* you feel like you've stumbled upon a treasure trove of relational wisdom and insight. But the real brilliance of the book is in how Chris provides tangible ways for us to apply that wisdom in our relationships. Like every master teacher, this gift was birthed out of his own journey, which makes you want to put it into practice—even the hard parts! Get ready to be challenged, encouraged and released to pursue everything God created you to experience out of your most significant relationships.

Alex Johnson, Pastor of Adult Discipleship, Highlands Community Church in Renton/Kent, WA

A Field Guide to Relationships is an excellent book that gives relationship strategies that actually work. It addresses one of the often-unaddressed topics of how Fleers and Flooders interact relationally, and the dynamics that creates. The chapter on boundaries is worth the price of the book. If you need strategies for addressing your relationship with your significant other, or want to take your relationship to the next level, then pick up this book today!

Elijah Stephens, author, pastor, professor, and Executive Producer of the upcoming film *Send Proof.*

It was a pleasure to read through *A Field Guide to Relationships*. I found myself smiling or wincing often because of how applicable and clear Chris' examples were! My favorite aspect is that Chris thoroughly covered every potential stage of a relationship: from laying a solid communication groundwork early-on by having realistic expectations to navigating life as divorced adults who still need to communicate effectively, he hits each scenario with thoughtfulness and thoroughness. You would be hard-pressed to find a person who wouldn't benefit from the work in this book. Thank you!

Matt Walker, President, Renew Transfer

A FIELD GUIDE TO
RELATIONSHIPS

OBSERVING HUMANS IN
THEIR NATURAL HABITAT

BY CHRISTOPHER T. ROGERS

PRUNE SEASON
Asheville, NC | 2019

For information, address the publisher at:
http://www.chrisrogerswrites.com/take-action
email chrisrogersmft@gmail.com
www.facebook.com/prayerfully.christopher

ISBN: 978-1-7313-9768-3

Editing and formatting by Caris Holliman.
Cover design by Daniel Hall.
Chapter images and author headshot by Mozingo Photography in collaboration with Chris Rogers.

To my family: Joy, Noah, and Miriam, you've given me the desire to achieve and to share with the world what we are learning together. Joy, you believed in me before I believed in myself.

"Heart to heart connection creates strength, and the tragedy is that we starve without it."

—Chris Rogers

"The greatest thing you'll ever learn is just to love and be loved in return."

—eden ahbez

CONTENTS

ACKNOWLEDGMENTS 11

A LITTLE ABOUT THE BOOK 13

INTRODUCTION 14

3 FOUNDATIONAL ELEMENTS................................16

INTRODUCTION REFLECTION QUESTIONS 19

TOOL #1 EACH PERSON CARRIES 50/50 RESPONSIBILITY............ 20

TOOL #1 REFLECTION QUESTIONS................... 23

TOOL #2 THERE ARE ALWAYS 2 THINGS HAPPENING AT ONCE 24

TOOL #2 REFLECTION QUESTIONS.................... 27

TOOL #3 FLOODING AND FLEEING.................... 28

TOOL #3 REFLECTION QUESTIONS.................... 35

TOOL #4 LIMITS (AKA: BOUNDARIES) 36

TOOL #4 REFLECTION QUESTIONS.................... 48

TOOL #5 COMMUNICATION 101..................... 50

TOOL #5 REFLECTION QUESTIONS.................... 58

TOOL #6 HARD, BROKEN, AND DISCONNECTED............ 60

TOOL #6 REFLECTION QUESTIONS.................... 63

TOOL #7 IDENTITY, ROLE, AND VALUE DEVELOPMENT............ 64

TOOL #7 REFLECTION QUESTIONS.................... 68

TOOL #8 LOVE IS A MIRROR.................... 70

TOOL #8 REFLECTION QUESTIONS.................... 74

TOOL #9 1, 2, 3, 4 HELP.................... 76

TOOL #9 REFLECTION QUESTIONS.................... 83

TOOL #10 FORGIVENESS (AND A LITTLE ABOUT TRUST) 84

TOOL #10 REFLECTION QUESTIONS.................... 87

IN CONCLUSION...88

CONCLUSION REFLECTION QUESTIONS.......................91

APPENDIX...93

ENDNOTES..96

ABOUT THE AUTHOR..97

ACKNOWLEDGMENTS

Joy Rogers, again thank you for your support as well as your "turtle" ways of looking at things, especially how to present the chapter questions.

Many thanks to my clients over the years for helping me to hone the images, concepts and tone of these pages.

Donna Austin, thank you for the first round of editing. You helped me get the ball rolling and asked questions to keep me focused.

Caris Holliman, you helped me capture my voice and challenged me to say what I mean. Thank you.

Mountain Mojo, you fueled my progress with relaxing atmosphere and coffee.

And Seacoast Asheville, thank you for the space, the opportunities, and the trust. You mean the world to me. Let's do this family thing more and more.

Mozingo Photography! A big thank you for the photo shoots and help creating picture templates.

Daniel Hall, your graphic design skills are fantastic, especially viewed side-by-side with my clip art. Thank you for taking the cover concept out of my mind and to the masses.

Finally, thank you to all who lent support, both emotionally and financially to this project. I hope it blesses you as much as you have blessed me.

A LITTLE ABOUT THE BOOK

PURPOSE: The purpose of this handbook is to give you 10 key tools to successful and fulfilling relationships. Consider it a field guide that lays out in simple terms what you need to know about fostering, creating, and sustaining real connection with the people in your life. This resource is for couples, friends, leaders, and parents alike.

STRUCTURE: Each section begins with a simple picture, a diagram, or a principle. On the following page or two max, an explanation of the picture or diagram will be communicated in straightforward, clear terms. At the end of each section, you will find a few reflection questions to be used for individual digestion or to facilitate a group discussion.

GOAL: Everything you need to create and sustain healthy relationships is in these pages. There is a lot that goes into a healthy relationship. This field guide has placed all of the pieces and parts to sustainable relationships in one place with the specific aim of application and usefulness. My hope is that you will be able to quickly read and retain the principles in each section without having to re-read a whole book. Practicality and application are what we often miss when seeking to learn and better ourselves.

INTRODUCTION

First and paramount, we must lay the best foundation for successful and sustainable relationships

A foundation is laid down before a structure can be built. The foundation holds up and stabilizes the structure. These 3 elements hold the 10 tools firmly in place, either giving us the ability to secure a relationship or, without them, to be in danger of it crumbling around us. If you want strong and lasting relationships you do not need a fresh coat of paint or new windows, you need a deep

INTRODUCTION REFLECTION QUESTIONS

1. Can you be honest with how often you offer genuine Love? What is it like?
2. When was the last time you experienced true freedom in a relationship?
3. What gets in the way of Connection for you?
4. What keeps you from getting back up after mistakes and moving forward to take appropriate risks in relationships?
5. Do you have a habit of cleaning up your own mistakes or do you tend to minimize their importance?

Notes:

TOOL #1 EACH PERSON CARRIES 50/50 RESPONSIBILITY

Move than (>)
50% is
TOO HEAVY

EQUAL PARTS RESPONSIBLE

Less than (<)
50% is
TOO LIGHT

TOOL #1
EACH PERSON CARRIES 50/50 RESPONSIBILITY

In every relationship, each person is fully responsible for themselves. Likewise, both parties are equally responsible for the success or failure of the relationship. In essence, "I'll do my part, and you are free to do, or not do yours." When we choose to love, we decide to do so independently of the other person's behavior, response, or reciprocity.

If you take < 50% you will feel justified for your actions and behaviors and do more waiting than proactively changing, forgiving, and healing.

If you take > 50% you will feel overburdened, overwhelmed, unlovable, and unable to work, heal, or change.

We never arrive in relationships.
Relationships are always in flux.

We are either moving toward intimacy and connection or away from it.

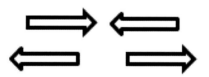

When you take on only your own 50% of the responsibility, you are doing your part to move toward the other person and toward connection.

Those brave enough to own their 50% start by seeing, accepting, and owning their part of the mess. People that are unable to start here at square one rarely do well with the rest of the tools. This doesn't mean the other person is innocent or that your pain doesn't matter. The fact is, you can only change you, so you must start with yourself. Over time you might *win* the right to influence the other person. When people do not feel the threat of harm or attack they will invite you in to share your hurts and issues.

DO NOT DEMAND IT.

When you overextend your rights by telling them what they are doing wrong, you will either get survival-mode compliance or defiant rebellion. In order for people to take in what you have to say, they need to be connected to you; they need to feel safe. Because of this it is best to start with cleaning up your side of the street and to wait until you are invited to help them with theirs.

TOOL #1 REFLECTION QUESTIONS

1. What do you expect your relationships to look like?
2. Are you doing your part to move toward love and connection?
3. Are you over-giving or under-giving to any relationships? Is there something holding you back from trusting yourself with people?

Notes:

TOOL #2 THERE ARE ALWAYS 2 THINGS HAPPENING AT ONCE

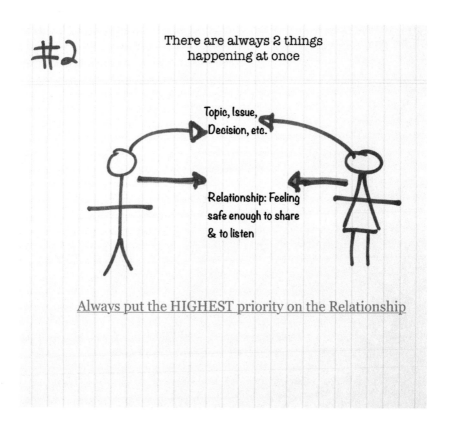

TOOL #2 THERE ARE ALWAYS 2 THINGS HAPPENING AT ONCE.

In every conversation, there are always 2 things going on at the same time.

1. The Topic/Issue/Decision at Hand
2. The Relationship

Think of a recent conversation you had with a spouse or friend. Reflect on the interaction by asking yourself this tool's essential question: **How did we experience each other: did we even settle the topic or just react to each other?**

What happens to you when you start to believe someone is mad at you or disappointed? How open and safe do you feel when your spouse gets angry? All of these emotions and our supplemental interpretations create a filter through which we hear and then take in information. For example, if I am feeling attacked or accused I will either **shut down**—closing myself off—or react and **attack** back. When you learn to attend to the relationship first and put the topic on hold when needed, you will experience more success in your communication.

Learn to cultivate connection with whomever you are speaking by attending to the relationship as the priority in your communication. This IS the practice of connection.

When one party in the relationship feels unsafe or threatened, their ability to hear, listen, and receive what is being said is diminished.

When an individual feels safe and valued, they will be more open and better able to see the best in what is being said.

Practice connecting on the level of relationship first, because the strength of the relational connection impacts how cleanly and clearly we will hear what's said in each conversation. There is always a filter between our ears and the speaker's words. A strong relational connection keeps that pathway unencumbered.

NOTE: If you find yourself getting hurt or offended, it is YOUR job to take a moment and attend to the relationship. Practice putting the topic/conversation on hold until safety has been re-established.

If you feel you are not being heard or respected, it is YOUR job to attend to the relationship. Again, respectfully refuse to progress in a conversation if you feel unsafe, attacked or <u>reactive</u> (especially if you are going to be reactive). Often, this means you will need to remove yourself from the room in order to maintain self-control. Simply communicate what you are doing, why you're doing it, and what you need to begin again. **This is not a power struggle.** This is you recognizing that you are no longer able to be fully present in the conversation, and as a result, the topic is unlikely to be successfully or respectfully resolved.

Relationship first. Get it?

TOOL #2 REFLECTION QUESTIONS

Use the first 3 columns of the following chart to look at how you handled an experience of anger or hurt. Then, use your answers to columns 4 & 5 to brainstorm ways you could improve your responses and behavior.

Situation?	What was your (internal) emotional response to the pain?	What was your outward reaction?	What was really happening/ what was really being said?	How could you have handled your emotions and needs differently?
1				
2				
3				

TOOL #3 FLOODING AND FLEEING

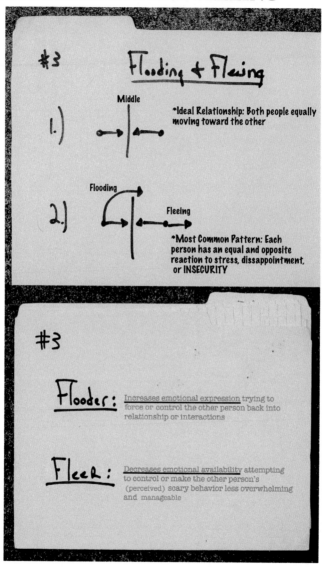

#3

Flooding + Fleeing

1.)

Middle

*Ideal Relationship: Both people equally moving toward the other

2.)

Flooding

Fleeing

*Most Common Pattern: Each person has an equal and opposite reaction to stress, dissappointment, or INSECURITY

#3

Flooder : Increases emotional expression trying to force or control the other person back into relationship or interactions

Fleer : Decreases emotional availability attempting to control or make the other person's (perceived) scary behavior less overwhelming and manageable

Tool #3 Flooding and Fleeing
Part 1

Your most recurrent behavior fits into one of these 2 categories, so don't fight it.

Be aware, be warned. Flooders find Fleers and Fleers seek out Flooders. We are just drawn to each other. The core question for this tool is: How does each person handle themselves or respond when they FEEL some version of **insecurity**?

What we are feeling may not be recognized as **insecurity** but something deep within feels:
    unsafe,
        unloved,
            unknown,
                devalued,
                    unimportant,
                        insufficient,
                          or overwhelmed.

The Flooder or Fleer pattern is a person's go-to reaction in most stressful situations. You might not <u>always</u> Flood or Flee, but when insecurity strikes, you will tend to deal with the fear using one of these trouble-shooting tactics.

How do you deal with the fear?

<u>**Flooders**</u> are very sensitive or aware of others' emotional **presence** or level of engagement. They are sensitive not only to physical presence, but also relational presence. When their insecurity (another's noticeable absence) is triggered, they begin to feel alone, unheard, or uncared for. The feeling of being alone causes them to believe they need to pull others into relationship or engagement.

Flooders do this by **increasing their emotional expression**— often without even realizing it. What they seek to create is a response, a reaction of any sort. They attempt to ease the fear of being alone by forcing a reaction or an entanglement. Flooders seek connection but tend to force or demand it. In extremes, Flooding can be seen as "negative attention is better than no attention." Or, as magical thinking: "If I am extra loving, caring, or even physical, will you like me more? Will you engage with me then?" By trying to force a reaction they often end up pushing or scaring people away— Flooding the relationship. In communication, Flooders often focus on a list of grievances or on the solution to a problem before being vulnerable and talking about how they feel.

Fleers are very sensitive to other's emotional and relational **volatility.** Fleers are overly aware of other people's needs. Fleers prioritize and work hard to create peace for those around them. Fleers' insecurity, therefore, is triggered by demands on their attention or feeling pressured to satisfy a need greater than they can fill. Their response tactic is to **decrease their emotional availability.** They check out. Fleers can be physically present but a million miles away. Fleers become skilled at evoking a look—or simulated experience—of presence and engagement, but over time, they begin to hide and disconnect from what is really going on inside themselves as well. They place such a high priority on others that they lose focus on themselves to an unhealthy extreme. They behave with the belief, conscious or otherwise, that "You matter. I don't. As long as you are happy I'll be just fine." The problem is that, increasingly, the Fleer's heart gets so hurt that they tend to harden and shut down. Without healthy communication, no one outside-looking-in knows why. Once a Fleer's heart becomes hardened, they leave those in their lives feeling rejected and as if there is limited option: let them go, leave them alone, or chase hard after them.

SUMMARY:
Both Flooders and Fleers fail to give helpful and safe information. Both avoid and fear genuine vulnerability.

Flooders:
List and critique without vulnerability.
They often come up with a solution to a problem that hasn't yet been identified or communicated to cover up their toxic feelings of loneliness. Focusing on solution before vulnerability can turn out more controlling than helpful.

Fleers:
Prioritize others to their own detriment.
They often seek to please and appease others for their own benefit (feelings of peace). The practice of peace-before-vulnerability is likely more selfish than chivalrous, more self-preservation than deliberate care for the connection.

Flooders often speak with intensity and outbursts while Fleers often keep quiet and cultivate silent resentments.

TOOL #3 FLOODING AND FLEEING
PART 2

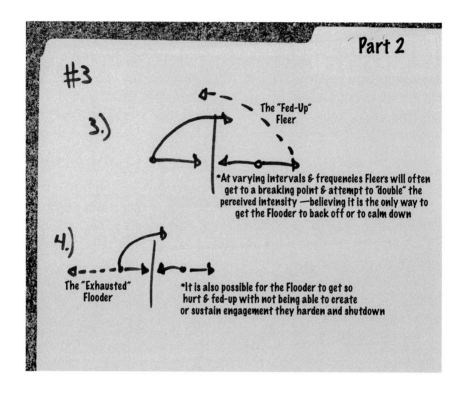

Part 2

#3

3.)

The "Fed-Up" Fleer

*At varying intervals & frequencies Fleers will often get to a breaking point & attempt to "double" the perceived intensity —believing it is the only way to get the Flooder to back off or to calm down

4.)

The "Exhausted" Flooder

*It is also possible for the Flooder to get so hurt & fed-up with not being able to create or sustain engagement they harden and shutdown

Tool #3 Flooding and Fleeing
Part 2

In all practicality, the Flooder and Fleer pattern is not always as simple as explained above. The first section described the basic patterns we all fall into, yet as a relationship progresses, the dance can get more complicated. Below we'll help clarify the second part of the dance. Now understand that this progression can take on a variety of shapes and variations. Some folks slip into the second part within a few weeks. Others won't witness this evolution until they've been married or in relationship for 15, 20, or 30 years. The movement from primary Flooder/Fleer into a secondary stage is the most common reason that relationships fall apart after years and years of time and experience. For married couples, it usually comes about shortly after the kids go off to college or move out. The marriage partners no longer have a strong common interest, and their bond starts to fall apart.

Fed-Up Fleer
The tragedy of the Fed-Up Fleer is that it takes a whole lot of courage to finally express pent up frustration. In essence, the Fed-Up Fleer is just temporarily Flooding. As you may guess, even in this outburst they are not expressing much helpful or intimate information. Factual information is lost due to the intensity. The message is further mixed when they quickly return to Fleeing and fail to follow through on what they have claimed is a solution. In this state, the Fed-Up Fleer expects everyone to understand them and becomes increasingly frustrated that people don't. As a result of Fleeing and putting a higher priority on others' needs, their heart is hardened to the natural processes of gradual change. The Fed-Up Fleer fails to notice a healthy shift when it begins, and continues to discourage and blame the Flooder. Unfortunately, this is usually when folks come into counseling. The Fed-Up Fleer opens the session with "I'm done. There is absolutely no hope for us." When this pattern

unfolds in a marriage, the spouse is usually dumbfounded and clueless.

Exhausted Flooder

Flooders crave engagement to feel secure. They need emotional and relational interaction as a platform for expressing their innate passion for life. If the Fleer is beautifully gracious and giving, then the Flooder is beautifully passionate and powerful. For Flooders, the downfall is in how they have used that raw power and energy to manipulate situations toward their chief aim: continual interaction. Eventually, some Flooders throw in the towel from emotional exhaustion. If Flooders cannot get enough of what they need or demand, some start to feel, "What's the point in even trying?" Tragically, the Exhausted Flooder thinks they have lost their natural depth of caring and no longer need interaction. In vain, they attempt to move on and are unaware that their heart remains emblazoned on their sleeve.

Their true condition of exhaustion shows in their actions and behavior. They tend to "do less" actively in the relationship, yet still Flood (even if it is with disappointment or disgust toward others). Because being passionate and powerful is the natural state of being for a Flooder, a Flooder usually has to make a very deliberate choice to direct that passion into receiving healthy feedback, in order for them to see accurately what their Flooding looks like. Regrettably, their very passion and strength consistently threatens to steamroll productive feedback. The more a Flooder resists feedback, the less self-aware they become. The best feedback is that which helps them see the cost of their behavior. They are often oblivious to how powerful or scary their passion appears, and how effective it is at reaching their desired outcome of connection—whatever the cost. Thus, when they throw in the towel, they believe they've given up for good. But their real and genuine need for connection can still rekindle and re-flood the relationship again and again.

TOOL #3 REFLECTION QUESTIONS

1. Do you have traits matching the description of Flooder or Fleer? What does it look like?
2. What are the signs and symptoms that your Flooding or Fleeing is beginning to increase?
3. What is one small thing you can do in your relationship this week to practice less Flooding or Fleeing?

TOOL #4 LIMITS (AKA: BOUNDARIES)
PART 1: LIMITS HELP ME, MANAGE ME.

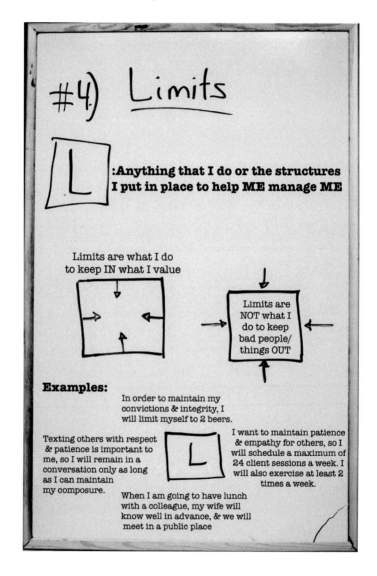

#4) Limits

L :Anything that I do or the structures I put in place to help ME manage ME

Limits are what I do to keep IN what I value

Limits are NOT what I do to keep bad people/ things OUT

Examples:

In order to maintain my convictions & integrity, I will limit myself to 2 beers.

Texting others with respect & patience is important to me, so I will remain in a conversation only as long as I can maintain my composure.

I want to maintain patience & empathy for others, so I will schedule a maximum of 24 client sessions a week. I will also exercise at least 2 times a week.

When I am going to have lunch with a colleague, my wife will know well in advance, & we will meet in a public place

Simply defined, Limits are anything that I do, or the structures that I put in place, to help ME manage ME.

ME MANAGE ME

I am the one who's responsible for me. I am a powerful and free person who can determine my own behavior. I need to consider what it takes to maintain and sustain myself for the long haul. Limits are how I do this. Limits are what I **do** to keep **in** what I **value**, says Danny Silk in *Keep Your Love On*.

If I want to maintain trust, integrity, and connection in my relationships, then I must intentionally structure my life to reflect these goals. We establish Limits to govern our lives, to cultivate that "best of me" toward others.

Example Limits

I will never have private and exclusive time with members of the opposite sex without my spouse's knowledge.

I will honor and respect my spouse even when he or she is not around.

I will take full charge of my attitudes and behavior. I am responsible or at fault if I don't manage me well.

If I run out of patience with my children, it is on me first *Ouch! *, if I value being patient with those I love.

I take time regularly to rest and meditate in order to maintain my own clarity.

I do not go into bars or to parties with lots of alcohol because I am committed to staying clear-headed about my sobriety.

I will not be alone or in private places with my boyfriend in order to keep my promise of purity.

I put my kids to bed at 8pm before I've run out of patience and am exhausted.

Because I cannot control anyone else, I must learn to manage me. Limits I make ensure that I keep to my convictions and my values. Limits are how I do my 50%—no more and no less—to nurture my relationships and my positive behavior.

Notes:

TOOL #4 LIMITS
PART 2

How and where I establish my limits must be governed by a HIGH value for others, as well as an equally HIGH value for myself.

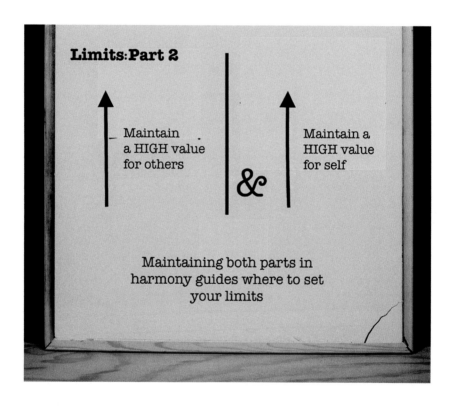

Limits: Part 2

Maintain
a HIGH value
for others

&

Maintain a
HIGH value
for self

Maintaining both parts in
harmony guides where to set
your limits

Limits Part 2
Limits are guided by my ability to maintain high value for self and for others.

High Value for Others: If my interactions and history with a person negatively impact my respect and patience for that person, then I need to set limits. The limit will help preserve my self-composure toward that person. Limits will reinforce for me how they deserve to be cared for or loved. When I get to the point of believing a person deserves less than respect or kindness—that they deserve a piece of my mind—then I have not managed myself well. **It is my job to "keep in" respect for others.** I cannot blame someone else if I start to believe that they deserve disrespect, and suddenly my respect for them bottoms out. I may need to set a limit on how often or how long I am around that person.

One of the most common applications for needing to establish limits to maintain a high value for others is in parenting. We often put more priority on being loved and liked than on our ability to be patient and non-threatening. Kids are not a new invention. They've been around for a long time. Their tantrums, emotional manipulation, and whining are not new tactics. Although difficult, we need to re-establish our limits and clarify our standards as parents. I hear regularly—I mean a <u>lot</u>—from kids about how scary or angry their parents are. And the parents usually refuse to see why their kids have a secret life. If you want your one-day 16-year-old to talk to you about sex, drugs, bullying, etc., then you must be patient and clear with your now 5-year-old at bedtime. We want to see these interactions as totally separate. Kids see them as a fluid experience. They are always learning whether you are going to manage you or if they should try to. They cannot manage you and be honest with you about scary information at the same time.

High Value for Self: If my experiences with a person cause me to lower my own value or to allow myself to be mistreated, then I need to set limits. For example, if I know that, historically, when I am with a particular friend I let their negative assessment of me define my value, then I need to limit the frequency and depth of our interactions. That is, I can set a limit on how much of me I will let them see and affect. Similarly, if I know that I've slowly allowed someone to treat me worse and worse over time, and I've begun to justify and take responsibility for their treatment of me, then I need to set limits on my interactions with that person.

Imagine that I am a friend of yours. My partner, on the other hand, you have learned to avoid. My partner tends to wield a big emotional bat over the people closest to them. Everyone who's anyone knows my partner is abusive, belittles others—really seeks out others' weakest points and drills into them. But I, your friend, keep walking into the bat. I cling to the abuse. In this example, my value for myself is off. MY limits are incorrectly set. Instead of hitting back one day because I can't take any more, I need to take a few steps back to renew my value for myself.

This type of limit is essential for those that find themselves in abusive or neglectful relationships. Undervaluation of self or others can happen at home, at work, or in the community. *(Search "Power and Control Wheel" as a guide for more information.)* Often those in abusive relationships are such great caretakers and/or such giving people that they tend to have a significantly disproportionate evaluation of their own needs and safety. In turn, they engage in, allow, minimize, or justify the undesirable behavior and treatment of others. The limits here are to facilitate **remembering** how you need and deserve to be treated. Again, the limits are not to make the abuse stop as much as to keep you fully cognizant of what is and is not appropriate. Trying to make the abuse stop is, in itself, controlling others. Without these limits, we find ourselves repeating the same patterns again, wondering how we got back into the abuse.

I tell people often that the number one profession that comes in to my office is: nurses. Or more generally: helping service-providers. Being natural caretakers, they automatically step up and care for others with ease. The problem is that they often do not implement self-valuing limits or enough self-care. These precious givers often have a diminished sense of their own value. In turn, they get into abusive and unsafe settings. And the sad part is that those closest to them in life rarely know that they feel this way. Occasionally getting upset does not clearly communicate as effectively as the consistency of behavior found in well set limits.

Important Note: WE ALL NEED PEOPLE. Yet, those we allow to speak into our lives need to be carefully selected, then gradually invited in over time, through positive experiences and the steady development of trust.

TOOL #4 LIMITS (AKA: BOUNDARIES)
LIMITS PART 3

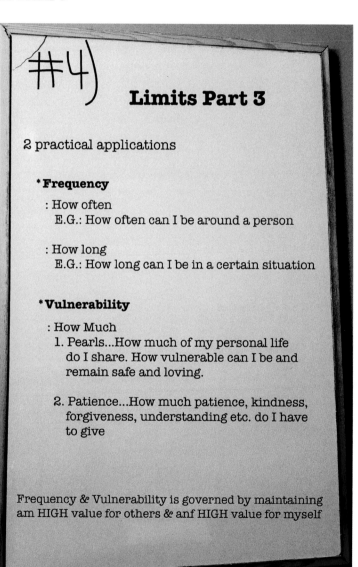

#4) Limits Part 3

2 practical applications

* Frequency

: How often
E.G.: How often can I be around a person

: How long
E.G.: How long can I be in a certain situation

* Vulnerability

: How Much
1. Pearls...How much of my personal life do I share. How vulnerable can I be and remain safe and loving.

2. Patience...How much patience, kindness, forgiveness, understanding etc. do I have to give

Frequency & Vulnerability is governed by maintaining am HIGH value for others & anf HIGH value for myself

Limits Part 3
Limits need to be practically applied.

How do I maintain a high value for others and a high value for myself? I do so by setting limits on both FREQUENCY and VULNERABILITY.

Frequency

In order to have a sustained value for both others and for myself I manage **How Often** and **How Long** I am in a situation or around a person.

o Limits are about me managing me. It is NOT about restricting, punishing, or avoiding others.
o I aim at giving the best of myself as much and as often as possible.
o I set limits on my frequency so that others experience the best of me as often as I can manage.
o Quality over quantity = improved self-control
o It is my job to remember to stick to my core values, beliefs, and standards.
o If I default to someone else's standards in order to maintain approval or to avoid conflict then I need to re-evaluate my limits.
o By not managing my frequency, I may lose focus on my value for self.

Vulnerability

First, understand that everything given to another person in relationship costs the giver. All relationships require give and take. Vulnerability deals with **How Much** I can give of my resources or how I manage what I have to give—most of which runs in a limited supply.

How Much I give in a relationship can be seen in 2 areas:

Pearls: How much intimacy and depth of my personal story I share. How vulnerable with my heart can I be and still maintain a High Value for you and a High Value for me? Pearls are rare and valuable. I can learn to give pearls in small incremental steps, establishing safety and trust.

Patience: How much patience, kindness, forgiveness, trust, and so on. Patience is just one example used to demonstrate the common elements of any relationship. These common elements cost the giver. And it is the giver's job to manage their limited supply.

o   I must learn to observe, reflect upon, and be honest with my experiences and my relational histories.
o   Positive and negative experiences impact how and where I set the limits of how much of me I am going to give.
o   I need to be giving to myself by respecting the prior levels of trust and safety I have experienced.
o   Physical and emotional intimacy are Pearls.

Note: As a by-product of well-established and maintained limits, some people in your life will start to ask how can they have <u>more</u>: more of your time or more depth in the relationship. If you were in a relationship that was increasingly demanding or decreasingly supportive, then start setting consistent limits. Some others will want to find out why you have changed. This is it! **This** is the moment when you can start to **communicate** what you need from them. We start by managing ourselves well, and then we move to communicating our needs for a better and stronger connection. Applying these principles in reverse order rarely works well. When you wait until they come to you to seeking more, you are more likely to get an active and engaged listener—a partner rather than a codependent.

TOOL #4 REFLECTION QUESTIONS

1. When do you tend to run out of patience or understanding? For example, at a regular time of day or with particular people?
2. Is there someone in your life to whom you need to limit the amount of time or energy that you give? What causes you to feel drained by these interactions?
3. What are the most rewarding relationships in your life? Is there a person or a group with whom you could take some risk to get to know even better?

Situation/ Relationship	What/how much of me am I giving?	How much do I have to give?	How do they respond in a way that makes this hard for me?	What can I change or do differently?
1				
2				
3				

Notes:

TOOL #5 COMMUNICATION 101
PART 1: WHAT IS SAID IS RARELY WHAT IS HEARD.

Tool #5 Communication 101
Part 1: What is said is rarely what is heard.

The most recurrent and common complaint in relationships is poor/ unsuccessful communication. We assume that if we're talking (and even agreeing), then our communication is successful. Unfortunately, this is rarely the case.

Communication = Commune

Communication happens when 2 or more people **commune,** or when they experience and understand each other. The challenge is putting a priority on listening & creating mutual understanding OVER making sure you are heard.
A common mistake is assuming that listening, validating, and understanding necessitates agreement. This isn't true. Listening and validating just means expressing respect and honor toward the other person. Your average person is hardwired to discern legitimate validation from counterfeits. Over time spent with unhealthy limits and daily lives showing no sign of slowing down, however, we can lose the knack. Let's get back to our basic instincts, back to the **commune**, with some easily-practiced survival tools.

The best way to create an environment where you are heard is to be a great listener.

TOOL #5 COMMUNICATION 101
PART 2: "I" VERSUS "YOU" STATEMENTS

Communication Survival Tool #1: **"I" Statements**

The first and most important communication tool is the use of "I" statements. Change your priority from telling others what they have or have not done (or what they should or should not do) and instead talk about your own experiences.

Unless someone has explicitly invited you to speak directly to them about themselves "You" statements almost always backfire. And even when folks say we can speak directly and plainly, that doesn't mean they are actually ready for it.

Keys:

"You" statements usually cause defensiveness and self-justification.
- It is possible to be factually accurate yet completely wrong at the same time.
- Love, honor, and respect need to supersede accuracy. (Even if you are Sherlock Holmes.)

"I" statements are difficult for a few simple reasons.
- "I" statements are more honest, more intimate, and more vulnerable. That's scary to most of us!
- We don't honor and respect our own heart and experiences enough to trust that others will do likewise. The temptation is to get self-critical instead of transparent. We put too high a priority on cultivating other's opinions.
- Truly successful communication (communing) differs greatly from what is modeled for us by seemingly successful people. Our basic human need to commune is at odds with getting ahead in our current social media-driven society.

TOOL #5 COMMUNICATION 101

Communication Survival Tool #2:
The Speaker/Listener Technique

What is said is rarely what is heard. Do not fight this. This is a communication reality best accepted on face value. Consider how often a text message or an email is wrongly interpreted. Whether through a media device or in person, we read into each other's meaning, filling in gaps, reading between the lines. We think, "Ooh, I know what you really mean."

We all assume that the closer the relationship and the greater the history, the higher the potential for successful and clear communication. In reality, experiences, disappointments, and hurt-places create filters through which we interpret or misinterpret what is said. This is why married people often get into cycles of fighting and unsuccessful communication. Each person reacts to their assumptions and interpretations of what is being said instead of learning to CHALLENGE ASSUMPTIONS.

After we misinterpret what is said, we react, we defend, or we justify our own actions and behaviors. We justify defensiveness, sarcasm, anger or even offense. And without even realizing what just happened, the original speaker does the same thing: they react to your reaction. This is the core of most fights. When we CHALLENGE ASSUMPTIONS, we can make sure we are mad for the right reasons before we fly off the handle in a fit of self-righteous behavior! Challenging assumptions in your communication is the perfect way to elevate the relationship over the conversation, to own your part, and to maintain a high value for both parties.

Key: In order to have sustainable, successful communication, both parties must take ownership.

1.<u>Speaker</u>: If you speak and the response does NOT seem to match your intended or assumed response.

*1st MAKE SURE THEY HEARD YOU AND UNDERSTOOD YOU BEFORE YOU REACT IN KIND.

2.<u>Listener</u>: When someone is talking to you and what they say hits you the wrong way, scares, offends, or confuses you.
*1st MAKE SURE YOU HEARD/UNDERSTOOD CORRECTLY BEFORE YOU REACT IN KIND.

The point is simple. We need to pause, to take just a moment to connect—to commune—with the person we're in communication with, before we trust our assumptions and interpretations. The practice is hard because it requires self-control and humility.

TOOL #5 REFLECTION QUESTIONS

1. Is there someone in your life who seems to repeat themselves often? If you take a minute to think about it, what do you believe they are trying to say?
2. What are 3 questions you could ask them to increase your understanding or to shift your view?
3. Write in your calendar or on a note to remind yourself every day for a week to ask the question, "Did I listen well today"? See if this intentionality makes a difference in your relationships.

Notes:

TOOL #6 HARD, BROKEN, AND DISCONNECTED

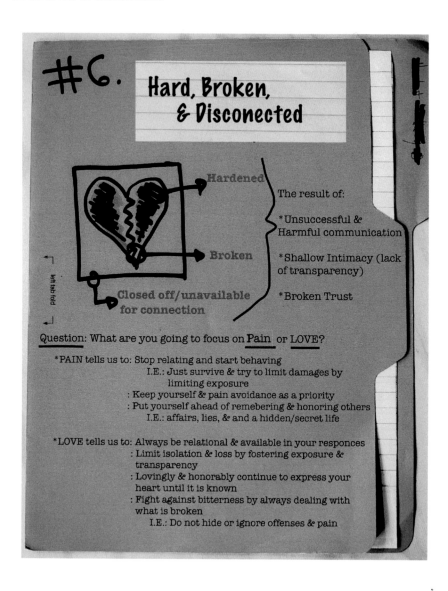

#6.

Hard, Broken, & Disconected

Hardened

Broken

Closed off/unavailable for connection

left tab fold

The result of:

*Unsuccessful & Harmful communication

*Shallow Intimacy (lack of transparency)

*Broken Trust

Question: What are you going to focus on **Pain** or **LOVE**?

*PAIN tells us to: Stop relating and start behaving
    I.E.: Just survive & try to limit damages by limiting exposure
    : Keep yourself & pain avoidance as a priority
    : Put yourself ahead of remebering & honoring others
      I.E.: affairs, lies, & and a hidden/secret life

*LOVE tells us to: Always be relational & available in your responces
    : Limit isolation & loss by fostering exposure & transparency
    : Lovingly & honorably continue to express your heart until it is known
    : Fight against bitterness by always dealing with what is broken
      I.E.: Do not hide or ignore offenses & pain

TOOL #6 HARD, BROKEN, AND DISCONNECTED

WARNING
→ Relationships are hard work.
→ You will get hurt and offenses are a part of the deal.
→ Your best bet is to develop the tools and the wisdom to DEAL with the issues WHEN they come, not if.
→ Your goal cannot be to avoid or eliminate issues and conflict.
→ Exposing what's going on inside = intimacy or "into-me-you-see" (You only see it if/because I showed it to you.)
→ Sex = the celebration of the work we have done to foster our connection.
→ Sex = the party, the enjoyment of the intimacy we have fought to protect and build.

The visual aid for this chapter is a picture of what happens to our hearts when we experience:

o   Unsuccessful or hurtful communication
o   Shallow intimacy
o   Broken trust

We have a choice to make, and we have to make it every day. In fact, we make this choice whether we intend to or not. We will be **loving** or we will be **selfish**. In matters of the heart—when it comes to intimacy—it is that black and white.

LOVE
→ is the proactive and intentional choice to move toward a person and to seek their best, alongside them. It is setting sights on that person's best, even when they are offering you their worst.
→ includes a willingness to risk more exposure as it is needed, in order to heal and forgive. Love deals with the hurt or offense until it is resolved, even when doing so causes some pain.

SELFISHNESS

→ is the act of self-preservation. Selfishness only considers self. Selfishness is the pattern or choice to "just survive" or to limit pain by hiding in plain sight.

→ hides the true condition of your heart, repeatedly giving in to the fear of more pain or rejection.

→ is the choice to protect your own best interests and your own needs or demands at the cost of, or without considering, others. It is the refusal to see a person beyond your own judgements, fears, or assumptions.

LOVE tells us to:

o Always be relational in our responses.

o Limit isolation by fostering exposure and transparency.

o (This means we have to set limits and cultivate a safe environment. In communicating our limits, we are actually being intimate and vulnerable, i.e. are valuing self and loving others.)

o Continue to express our hearts until they are known, until we are truly seen.

o Always honor others. Do not let dishonor breed dishonor.

o Fight against bitterness by always dealing with what is broken. (More on forgiveness later.)

TOOL #6 REFLECTION QUESTIONS

1. What is the greatest challenge to your most important relationship?
2. What causes you to shift from selfless to selfish, or from giving and open to self-preservation?
3. Love is a risk. What are you willing to risk for the possibility of gaining a better relationship?

TOOL #7 IDENTITY, ROLE, AND VALUE DEVELOPMENT

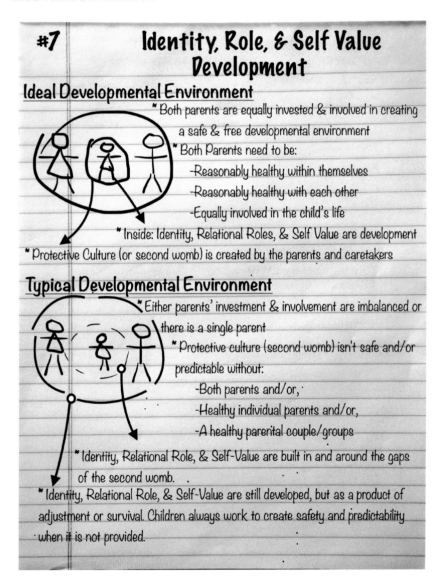

#7 **Identity, Role, & Self Value Development**

Ideal Developmental Environment

* Both parents are equally invested & involved in creating a safe & free developmental environment

* Both Parents need to be:

  -Reasonably healthy within themselves

  -Reasonably healthy with each other

  -Equally involved in the child's life

* Inside: Identity, Relational Roles, & Self Value are development

* Protective Culture (or second womb) is created by the parents and caretakers

Typical Developmental Environment

* Either parents' investment & involvement are imbalanced or there is a single parent

* Protective culture (second womb) isn't safe and/or predictable without:

  -Both parents and/or,

  -Healthy individual parents and/or,

  -A healthy parental couple/groups

* Identity, Relational Role, & Self-Value are built in and around the gaps of the second womb.

* Identity, Relational Role, & Self-Value are still developed, but as a product of adjustment or survival. Children always work to create safety and predictability when it is not provided.

TOOL #7 IDENTITY, ROLE, AND VALUE DEVELOPMENT
(AKA We all have baggage.)

For children:

```
Consistency = Predictability

    Predictability = Safety

        Safety = Freedom to be me
```

The need for a womb-like experience does not end just because the child is born. Children continue to need a safe and nurturing environment in which to grow and to develop until about the age of twelve. The family unit, home, and community of a child establish this "second womb," where we develop emotionally, relationally, and psychologically. While in development, these parts of a person are just as fragile in an average five-year-old as the spinal cord is in a five-month-old fetus. Instead of developing eyes, ears, and toes we are developing our own IDENTITY, our sense of SELF-VALUE, and an understanding of our ROLE IN RELATIONSHIPS.

Ideally, we are all given a safe, free, and reassuring environment for our development to be fostered. Most of our parents worked hard to provide the best possible environment. Yet, in over 12 years of experience in the helping services, I have yet to meet a single person who experienced the fully ideal environment.

Baggage: we all have it, and we all know it. Our early years affected us, and perhaps more than we want to admit. We may have passed the legal age of adulthood or have been married for 40 years, but still haven't taken ownership of how we are coping. As adults, we are free to continue blaming our parents for how we are living at 20, 30, or 70 years old. Ignoring this reality is called DENIAL. Justifying our behavior or lack of growth—to the point of being stuck in this reality—is called being a VICTIM.

In brief, we are all shaped by both "mothering" and "fathering," both masculine and feminine interactions. Without both, or with limited exposure to one of these gender expressions, our own sexuality and our understanding of our ROLE IN RELATIONSHIP is affected.

We need our parents/caregivers to be at least reasonably healthy within themselves *and* at least reasonably healthy with each other. Kids tend to try to fill in the gaps where their parents or primary caregivers are not healthy within themselves or with each other. In and of itself, kids helping out the family sounds reasonable, but the problem is that their earliest sense of IDENTITY and their SELF-VALUE is being formed by repeated interactions and experiences. The family culture shapes IDENTITY and SELF-VALUE.

For example: If Dad is an angry alcoholic, and kids need safety in their environment, then they will take on the job of creating safety for themselves, generally by trying to manage Dad's behavior for him. Fully managing other people's behavior is impossible. The kids' sense of IDENTITY and SELF-VALUE is now being shaped by a situation which is beyond their capacity to succeed in. Without help and healing they will unfortunately either marry someone with a similar need to be managed (co-addict/codependent) or become someone who needs to be managed (addict/codependent).

If an ideal environment is not established and maintained for a child, the child will take on some level of responsibility to attempt to create it for themselves. Unfortunately, their understanding or interpretation of what is best is only informed by their short lifetime's experiences.

They end up encouraging or facilitating the very problems they hope to eliminate.

o   Either they conform to the expectations and situation, feeling responsible to maintain normalcy,
o   Or they feel defeated and their feelings of powerlessness push them to rebel against the "second womb gone wrong".

The skills developed in childhood, cultivated over time, become how we understand our ROLE IN RELATIONSHIPS. And, if we are not careful, if we do not heal, we then seek and foster a version of these experiences in our adult relationships.

The point of this section is to simply help YOU understand YOU a little better.

Situations do not create internal condition. Situations expose internal condition.

How you respond to hurt and disappointment tells us more about YOU and YOUR past than it does about your spouse, partner, co-worker, friend, or the guy that just cut you off in traffic.

People often say, "What's the point?!? I can't change my past!" This is true, but you can come to a better understanding of how you interpreted these experiences, and, by doing so, let your IDENTITY, your SELF-VALUE, and your ROLE IN RELATIONSHIPS heal and change. What could you do with a stronger IDENTITY, SELF-VALUE, and ROLE IN RELATIONSHIPS?

TOOL #7 REFLECTION QUESTIONS

1. What do you know about your childhood that shaped you in positive and negative ways?
2. Was there a time in your childhood when you felt unsafe or uncared for? How did that affect you?
3. What coping skills did you acquire from your developmental years that may not serve you well as an adult? What positive skills have you developed in your life?

Notes:

TOOL #8 LOVE IS A MIRROR

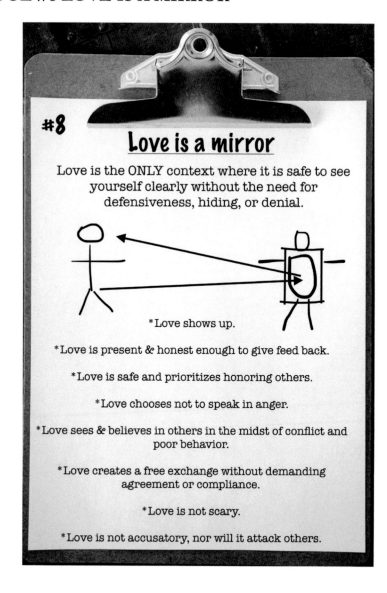

#8

Love is a mirror

Love is the ONLY context where it is safe to see yourself clearly without the need for defensiveness, hiding, or denial.

*Love shows up.

*Love is present & honest enough to give feed back.

*Love is safe and prioritizes honoring others.

*Love chooses not to speak in anger.

*Love sees & believes in others in the midst of conflict and poor behavior.

*Love creates a free exchange without demanding agreement or compliance.

*Love is not scary.

*Love is not accusatory, nor will it attack others.

TOOL #8 LOVE IS A MIRROR

Love is the only context where it is safe to see yourself. Love is a mirror. In this mirror, we are truly at rest; we are finally peaceful enough to see ourselves, without the need to self-preserve, hide, or defend.

We can see ourselves because we are not fearful, nor are we being attacked. Self-reflection arises also because love shows up. Love gives us feedback. We need love as a point of contact to be able to examine ourselves. When there's no feedback there's rarely genuine love.

Love is the safest context for me to see myself and my own behavior. It is likely the only place where I will take IN what you have to say and see where it fits. Love will help me to realize "I don't want you to feel alone. I want to do something about that."

By the same token, however, the feedback can be as factually accurate as you can muster, but if I do not feel loved, if I do not feel safe in the relationship, if the interaction moves me from peace to insecurity or fear—then I only see you. As my father-in-law warned us almost 20 years ago, "It is not what you say. It is how you say it." There is a dynamic difference between helpful/receivable feedback and criticism. Love isn't critical; it is inviting. Love isn't scary; it is safe.

Without love: I see your behavior not mine or I don't see anything because you forgot to show up

Lost that loving feeling? Don't know who this person is in the mirror? You've probably forgotten the keys for healthy communication. A "you" statement will only cause me to defend or excuse my behavior.

This is where "I" statements work beautifully.
- o I feel alone. vs. You don't care about me.
- o I'm scared and feel attacked. vs. You're a jerk
- o I need you to come and talk to me. vs. You aren't listening to me.

Love is a MIRROR is where most relationships suffer and fail. Consider carefully: If you don't say it, don't say it often, and/or don't say it lovingly, then others have no idea what you want, need or feel. No one is a mind reader. No one is wired to take in toxic, scary or accusatory information.

Love is a MIRROR is the only way successfully to create healthy and sustainable change without using the catalyst of fear, intimidation, or demanded compliance.

The idea that "they should know what I mean by now" is a nonstarter. Either they understand you, or they don't. You either have their heart and attention on a given issue, or you don't.

Give up: "They should know by now."
Embrace: "I will keep communicating until we've created our new normal together."

Once you've begun to see yourself in the mirror of love, you have the freedom to choose what to say, and what to do. The receivable feedback helps you see what you want to change by letting you see how you are being experienced. We must remain open, in fact, we must seek feedback. Feedback is how we grow. Responding to feedback is how we demonstrate our willingness to heal and change. When you stop using the mirror's feedback on your issues, then you have effectively stopped communicating the message "Change Needed" and have reverted to "Nothing's wrong here. Continue as planned." Refusing feedback is the equivalent of saying, "I choose myself over you. I don't want to change, nor do I want to improve my love for you."

Remember that an important part of a quality relationship is learning to talk about HOW we talk to each other. This can mean that we talk about the mirror and whether or not we are able to hear and receive each other. Talking about the mirror is intimacy in itself.

Key: Love trusts love as the best course of action even if it didn't seem to work at first. In fact, effective communication usually takes time, practice, and patience.

TOOL #8 REFLECTION QUESTIONS

1. In what relationships do you tend toward "You" statements?
2. Use the chart to look at your frequent "You" statements and then write a corrective "I" statement to replace it.

Typical "You" Statement	Replacement "I" Statement

Notes:

TOOL #9 1, 2, 3, 4 HELP

#9: 1, 2, 3, 4 HELP

KEYS

- You can only HELP someone who has (or recognizes) a problem.
- You can only HELP someone once you've been INVITED to do so. You must be asked to HELP.

┌── **STEP FOUR**

Asking you for HELP: Once they start asking questions & inviting you to HELP, process one small pearl at a time. First giving some reflective questions and small suggestions.

┌── **STEP THREE**

Open to you: They are receptive to building rapport, including hearing you talk about you... one pearl at a time.

┌── **STEP TWO**

Loved by you: Understood as... "You are free to be you around me." Love that is not conditional on behavior nor measurable change.

┌── **STEP ONE**

Safe with you: No threat of harm or punishment, either real or assumed.

NOTE: The order of steps is intential to build up toward HELP.

TOOL #9 1-2-3-4-HELP

We all have people in our lives who need help. It might be a friend or a child, a spouse or a parent, but we all have someone. There are a series of common questions that go something like:

"How do I help my _____ (son, husband, friend, etc.) with his/her addiction?"
"How do I make my wife understand what I need in our relationship?"
"How can I make it clear to my husband that he works too much?"
"Why won't my daughter let me help her?"
"Why does she cut herself and hide it from me?"
And on and on and on…

The steps to **helping** someone are easy to understand but difficult to keep in order. We <u>all</u> want to start with helping someone, forgoing the need to first be asked or invited in to help. (Remember 50/50; ME manage ME?)

The matter is complicated further because, offhand, people say they want help but aren't ready to take in what help is being offered. Most of us do not understand and appreciate the simple hierarchy of human needs: first to feel safe, then loved, followed by a willingness to observe and outline our actual problems. Once we are willing to see the problem, we are then open to Love is a MIRROR.

The illustration is of steps building upward. The steps must be established one on top of the other, in order. Each step must remain intact in order to move forward. If, say, step 1 is compromised, but you've been working on step 3, you are now back at step 1. Any attempt to fight this natural building process is counterproductive. You may get compliance, but you will not get real and genuine change.

TOOL #9 1-2-3-4-HELP

The 4 STEPS

1) SAFE with you

The person must believe they are SAFE with you and not under any threat of harm or punishment.

The person must believe that you are in connection with them, free of requirements to change and without an agenda.

The person must believe that you are for them and not against.

Connection comes before correction.

If practiced well, this will already be in place when correction becomes necessary.

2) LOVED by you.

Your mutual understanding is: "you are free to be you around me."

The person must believe your priority is to care for them, to love them as they are, and not to push them to change or correction.

*At this step, it is still all about the person being helped. You are there to listen and even to comfort when possible.

Remember that listening DOES NOT necessitate agreement or condoning unhealthiness. You are agreeing that the person needs love, not necessarily ascending to what they are saying, or believing.

Often you must look past the behavior of the person here. To maintain integrity of step 1, you might need to set limits around your ability to create a SAFE place and to LOVE them. If you cannot do this, then you are NOT the one to help create change.

Again, if the other relationship tools and keys are practiced well, then step 2 will already be in place when correction is needed.

3) OPEN to you

Once steps 1 and 2 are in place you can begin to talk about yourself.

In order to successfully work through step 3 you must maintain steps 1 and 2 (SAFE and LOVED).

Talking about yourself means using "I" statements

EX:
"I've always struggled being patient when it took a long time to change something about myself."
"I know myself enough to know I cannot drink that much anymore."
"Man, that sounds really tough to me."

You are NOT trying to change, fix, or manipulate them. You are just sharing from your own stories.

Once this seems to go well (and they still feel SAFE and LOVED) then you can start to talk about how their behavior affects you or others.

EX:
"It scares me when I don't hear from you for a few days."
"I often feel alone when you are gone."
"I cannot stay calm when I'm being yelled at, so I tend to shut down."
"I do not feel safe with the choices being made."

In this exchange—with you sharing about yourself first—the other person is getting a FREE opportunity to see themselves without feeling under a microscope.

It is here that people are most likely to see the need to change or at least look at the problems.

This is LOVE as a MIRROR.

Their response to you talking about yourself tells you how OPEN, SAFE and LOVED they feel with you.

<u>4) ASKING for HELP</u>

A by-product of being SAFE and LOVED, and then encountering you as OPEN in the relationship: People start to experience the MIRROR and see themselves, unguarded.

Without being judged or punished, people are more likely to not only ASK, but be willing to pursue further levels of HELP.

DO NOT jump in headlong!

Slowly begin to help, direct, and encourage—one "pearl" at a time.

The "win" is when you are brainstorming together.

Your best HELP is directing people toward cleaning up their own messes and troubleshooting their own solutions.

Common Mistakes

We all want to create change BUT we all want to control the process.

NOTES:

o   Real and sustainable change is only possible through a free exchange of mutual respect.

o   Parents and bosses alike want to ASSUME their authority gives them the necessary position to offer receivable direction, without fail.

o   Partners and spouses ASSUME steps 1 and 2 are a given.

o   Honoring these steps creates sustainable change.

o   Real change is different than conformity.

o   Fear is a great initiator, but it has no finish.

TOOL #9 REFLECTION QUESTIONS

1. With whom do you feel the safest? How open are you in those relationships?
2. What are the qualities and the nature of a safe relationship?
3. Where do you tend to start off when trying to "Help" people?
4. What mistake or assumptions do you make when "Helping?"

Notes:

TOOL #10 FORGIVENESS (AND A LITTLE ABOUT TRUST)

#10 Forgiveness

★ Healthy relationships practice forgiveness regularly, often daily.

★ We actively forgive in order to keep our heart free from being cut off, broken, & hardened.

★ We actively forgive because it is the only way to remain willing to take risks and to practice connection.

• <u>Forgiveness is letting go of my rights to or demand for:</u>

→ <u>Justice</u>—Withholding love until the debt has been made right or settled. The offender must restore what was broken without help or love.

→ <u>Punishment</u>—Withholding love until the offender has suffered "enough" for their crimes. The offender has to pay for their crimes.

→ Waiting until they "<u>get it</u>"—Withholding love until the offender "fully understands what they have done." The offended person is waiting to "feel better" & is usually waiting for the offender to serve both Justice & Punishment (NOTE: This is where most of us get stuck.)

TOOL #10 FORGIVENESS (AND A LITTLE ABOUT TRUST)

Healthy and fulfilling relationships practice forgiveness regularly, often daily.

If you cannot forgive, then you cannot give, nor can you receive, love.

If you refuse to forgive, you are choosing to disconnect and work on self-preservation instead of intimacy.

A VERY common misunderstanding is that, when we forgive, we have immediately and completely restored trust. In real life, this is rarely true.

Trust is a separate issue.

Trust is not reestablished simply by the hurt person's choice to forgive.

Trust is built through the repeated experience of safer and healthier behavior by the "offender"—the person who was experienced as scary, unpredictable and/or harmful.

Re-establishment of trust = Time ^{X} New experiences of a consistently-demonstrated, healthier standard of behavior

Forgiveness, on the other hand, is the intentional decision not to seek to harm or to punish the offender. Inherent in forgiveness is the humble understanding that you are no better and no worse than the offender. Your behaviors may be different, but you too can be scary, unpredictable and/or selfish. In fact, refusing to forgive and insisting on punishment is scary.

Forgiveness is a humanitarian act. We all want it, and we all need it. Just ask the state trooper, the school teacher, or the guy next to you in traffic. Wherever there is a refusal to forgive and insistence on punishment, there is fear, prejudice, and suffering.

When is forgiveness needed?
o   When you are hesitant to connect, share, or be intimate.
o   When you find yourself tempted to withhold love and affection. (**Withholding**, the opposite of setting **limits,** is an act of punishing and of seeking to harm.)

Unforgiveness causes us to hide, self-protect, and self-preserve. **Forgiveness** renews your willingness to **risk,** and all relationships require **risk** in order to grow.

Troublesome reality
Every time the initial wound is pricked or poked, you are introduced to a new opportunity to forgive until trust is fully re-established.

You can go days, weeks, or years, even, practicing forgiveness, and then get re-introduced to the broken trust and need to choose forgiveness again.

I've heard it said, "You never forgive. You are always forgiving."

TOOL #10 REFLECTION QUESTIONS

1. Do you have resistance to, or are you guarded with, a certain person?
2. If so, who is this person? What feelings are producing the resistance?
3. Ex. Every time you see your boss, you get anxious or defensive.
4. Are there specific topics that worry you or are scary to discuss?
5. Do you find yourself having an internal dialogue where you imagine you already know how the other party will answer or respond? Who? Explain.
6. The next time you see this person, write down how you feel about them. Ask yourself if you can begin to forgive this person. Begin to see how you could extend love while being honest with the level of trust you have experienced. Practice and repeat.

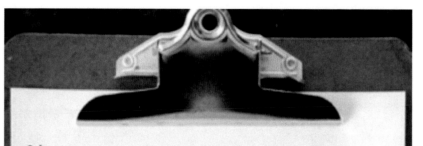

Notes:

IN CONCLUSION

We are relational by nature. We cannot live without relationships. Marriages and family relationships can be the safest place on earth. Relationships and family are where we learn, heal, risk and grow. They are the place from which we step out into life. And, safe places do not happen by accident! They must be carefully and intentionally crafted—then cultivated, in and out of season, for better or worse, for richer or poorer.

I always have hope, and I always see the potential for positive change. Always. Not only am I always a "glass half-full" kind of guy, I have now met with thousands of people in well over a decade of experience. Anything is possible. I want this to encourage you. Don't be discouraged by struggles and setbacks; they are a part of the gig. You can heal, and you can change, and so can your partner, your family, and your friends. It just takes work. Accept that your relationships won't ever be perfect, but the pursuit of excellence and an appreciation for improvement will go a long way.

The question is not: "Can we work this out?" The question you must ask yourself is: "Will we commit to the work and learning, to create the change necessary for success?" Use this Field Guide to help you through the process, through the time, work, and confusion that creating change produces. Each of the 10 sections have been carefully curated for your benefit. When you get stuck or hit an impasse, refer back to these pages for review. And, embrace the benefits of a successful counselor or therapist when needed. If in trouble, get help. This book is a resource and a guide, not the cure.

Change is always possible, but remember that change always starts with you. You are responsible for you. To do your part, you must independently choose and re-choose the other person in the midst of their pain and poor behavior. Guard your hope, keep it safe, and operate from hope toward others. This is what love does. This is what love looks like. Genuine love is passionate and committed to the process.

CONCLUSION REFLECTION QUESTIONS

1. What relationships in your life need some work?
2. What can you do to improve the level of safety and trust in these relationships?
3. Can you be honest with your 50% in relationships? What are the most common negative attributes you bring into relationships?
4. What do you want in your relationships? What is your expectation for changing your part of the relationship? Talk to a trusted friend or professional to see if your expectations are realistic.

Notes:

APPENDIX

Let's talk about your options in marriage.

<u>Warnings from Professional Experience:</u>

Sometimes the D word (Divorce) is a reality. BUT, please understand that divorce is not really the end of the relationship. In fact, if there are kids involved, it is only **the re-negotiation of a relationship.** Divorce does not miraculously create respect, self-control, and good communication. So, divorce can be the opportunity to work on your part of change, even if others refuse. Countless numbers of people have tried to convince me that their only option is divorce. It is not the only option but it is **an** option. I do not judge anyone for their life or their choices. (I've done too much of my own therapy, and I have too much of a shady past to play judge.) I have worked with many folks starting with marriage therapy and then finished by walking them through divorce. I care for all my clients the same. I am only saying the idea that divorce will make your life easier is rarely—and I mean rarely—the reality. Divorce is the choice of a specific course of difficulties away from and independently of your spouse. But your troubles have one very common element: you. You are everywhere you go. If marriage is one path with its serious collection of difficulties, then divorce is a different path with a similar set of difficulties. If there are no children, then you still have to deal with the hurt and casualties on your own. And, whatever your 50% was in the marriage goes with you. You are blessed with the ability to make your own choices. Know that I bless you to make your own choices in marriage and divorce.

One of my less than romantic, but accurate thoughts: we are all attracted, above everything else, to mutual dysfunction. We are all most attracted to our equal and opposite dysfunctional self. Less clinically, we all know that "opposites attract." We like to think we chose our partner based on some attraction and romantic notions. I suggest to you that we pick our partners because they are the other half of our own complex dysfunction. They are the Flooder to our Fleer, the "I'll take less than 50 percent if you'll take more than 50 percent."

We all look for someone to partner with in our own unique form of neediness.

Here's my point: getting divorced doesn't fix or change your unique type of neediness. Odds are, after divorce you will find a new but similar Flooder or Fleer to partner with. I have met several folks on their 2nd, 3rd or 4th marriage (my record is 5th but I've heard of 2 different people on their 7th) look at me dead in the eye and ask the same question: "How does this keep happening to me? Why do I keep marrying the same person?" My answer is, "Your picker is broken." If you do not change or heal, then you are still attracted to the same type of dysfunction. You still have to wake up with yourself. Divorce is a geographical solution to a psychological problem.

You forgot to learn from the brokenness and the mistakes of your 1st or 2nd attempt at marriage. If not marriage, then examine your friendships, or employment, or church. As you heal, grow, and change you will in turn be attracted to healthier people. Those who have been successful in their 2nd or 3rd attempts know what I am talking about. Those who have successfully overcome addiction know exactly what I am talking about.

At age 19, I moved from Massachusetts to Georgia for college, but inside I was looking for a fresh start. I was a major pot-head and took advantage of anyone I could find. At my university orientation, I met a guy. We skipped orientation to go smoke a joint. We arranged to be roommates. I spent the next 2 years drunk, high, tripping, popping pills, and going to raves in the shady parts of downtown Atlanta. I had changed my location, but not my internal compass. I learned, I believe we all have to stop running and start dealing with ourselves.

Lastly, I want you to know that YOU can create change in your life. You can. Do not wait or hesitate until others in your life get on board or take the lead. You do it. You do it for you. Do it for the kids, man, the kids! Learning to love, communicate, and forgive well will be to your own gain. You are the company you keep. As I have said to hundreds of couples, "I promise you that I can help you create change in your life and in your relationships. I just can't promise that your partner will come with you. But it is clear that it is time, and that change is needed.

ENDNOTES

Silk, D. (2015). Keep Your Love On: Connection, Communication & Boundaries. United States: Loving on Purpose.

ABOUT THE AUTHOR

Christopher T. Rogers trained in Marriage and Family Therapy at Richmont Graduate University and in Bible and Theology at Lee University. As a therapist and freelancer in the helping services for more than 12 years, Chris has helped people from many walks of life to bridge the gap between emotional/relational pain and healthful wholeness, both in their relationships and in their spirituality. Chris resides in the Western North Carolina mountains with his wife, Joy, and their two children. He hopes this guide proves a useful tool as you're learning to navigate the wilds of human connection.

GET CONNECTED

If you enjoyed *A Field Guide to Relationships*, there is plenty more to learn!

Visit me at www.chrisrogerswrites.com where you can:
- o Get notified of new book releases or upcoming speaking engagements.
- o Book a 20-minute counseling consultation, in person or via video conference.
- o Schedule your own event appearance or a corporate team consultation.
- o Arrange collaborations with other authors or speakers.

Workshops and counseling are my true passion. Let's talk about how I could serve your church, business, or family. Honest reviews and questions about the book are, of course, welcome.

I'd love to hear from you!

Email chrisrogersmft@gmail.com or message facebook.com/prayerfully.christopher.